CRASHED US PLANE WAS ON AUTOPILOT

'GOOGLE PHONE' BUILDS MOMENTUM

MONKS MAKE TEMPLE OUT OF BEER BOTTLES

CHARITIES NOW SEEK BANKRUPTCY PROTECTION

MICROSOFT'S IPHONE RIVAL NICKED

STUDY FINDS POSITIVE OUTLOOK GENE

UNITED NATIONS FOIL PIRATE ATTACK

EARLIEST HUMAN FOOTPRINTS FOUND

MINISTER CALLS FOR SUMO DOPING TEST

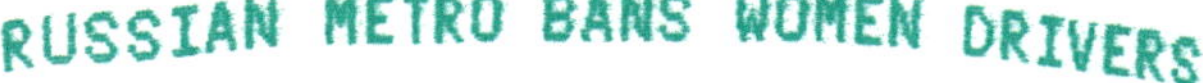
RUSSIAN METRO BANS WOMEN DRIVERS

SOMALI PIRATES RELEASE EGYPTIAN SHIP

NEWCASTLE 1-2 MANCHESTER UNITED

ARCTIC SUMMER ICE COULD VANISH BY 2013

A BURGLAR? NO, IT'S A KANGAROO

INEQUALITY IS BAD FOR YOUR HEALTH

CHINA AIMS TO REGROW ITS 'EMPTY FORESTS'

GIRLS DO BETTER WITHOUT BOYS

SUSTAINABILITY IS BACK IN FASHION

CRABS 'CAN REMEMBER SUFFERING PAIN'

JOBLESS WORKERS PAID TO LEAVE JAPAN